My Father's House
Nazarene Missions in Samoa

2001-2 NWMS
MISSION EDUCATION RESOURCES

❋ ❋ ❋

READING BOOKS

BY THE GRACE OF GOD
The Life of Grace Prescott
by Della Hines Newnum

IF MY PEOPLE
The Manny Chavier Story
by Steve Adams

JOURNEYS OF FAITH
From Canada to the World
by Valerie J. Friesen

MISSION IN THE THIRD MILLENNIUM
by Chuck Gailey

MY FATHER'S HOUSE
Nazarene Missions in Samoa
by Francine Duckworth and Nancy Fuga Stephenson

TO THE ENDS OF THE EARTH
Proclaiming the Gospel Through the *JESUS* Film
by L. David Duff

❋ ❋ ❋

ADULT MISSION EDUCATION RESOURCE BOOK

CALLED TO ALL NATIONS
Edited by Wes Eby

My Father's House

Nazarene Missions in Samoa

by
Francine Duckworth
and
Nancy Fuga Stephenson

Nazarene Publishing House
Kansas City, Missouri

Copyright 2001
by Nazarene Publishing House

ISBN 083-411-8440

Printed in the
United States of America

Editor: J. Wesley Eby

Cover Design: Michael Walsh

All Scripture quotations are taken from the King James Version
of the Bible (KJV).

10   9   8   7   6   5   4   3   2   1

Dedication

To my husband, Larry,
and our children—Deborah, John,
James, and Danelle—
who many times helped me stay in Samoa
when I wanted to leave.

To the many Samoans
that are part of our spiritual family
around the world.
We think of you often, pray for you much,
and miss you terribly.

Fa'amamuia le atua ia te outou! God bless you!

—Francine Duckworth

To my father, Selaga Fuga,
who encouraged me to go to
Bethany Nazarene College
and helped me spiritually and financially.

—Nancy Fuga Stephenson

American Samoa

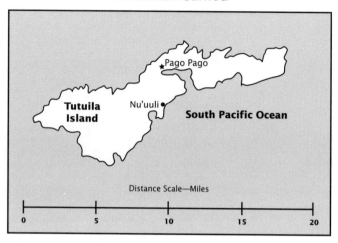

Pago Pago

Nu'uuli •

Tutuila Island

South Pacific Ocean

Distance Scale—Miles

| | | | | |
|0|5|10|15|20|

Samoa
(formerly Western Samoa)

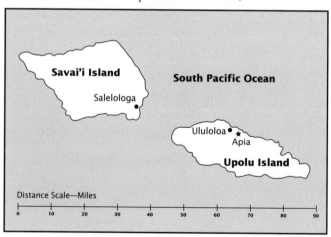

Savai'i Island

South Pacific Ocean

Salelologa •

Ululoloa • ★ Apia

Upolu Island

Distance Scale—Miles

0 10 20 30 40 50 60 70 80 90

Contents

Francine Duckworth and her husband, Larry, were Nazarene missionaries in American and Western Samoa from 1977-97. The Duckworths now live in Brush, Colorado, where they pastor the Church of the Nazarene. They have four children: Deborah, John, James, and Danelle. Francine has written for *World Mission* magazine and *Come Ye Apart* devotional guide.

Nancy Fuga Stephenson was the first Samoan to graduate from a Nazarene college and return immediately to minister to her own family and people. Presently living in California with her husband, Joe, she works for the INS (Immigration and Naturalization Service). For six years she pastored the Santa Ana Samoan Church of the Nazarene. The Stephensons have four children: Leilani, Christopher, Sapela, and Teanna.

The coauthors began to bond when they first met in Samoa in June 1977. The two women became spiritual sisters, and over the past quarter of a century they have encouraged each other in their walk of faith. Two of their daughters, Leilani (Nancy's) and Danelle (Francine's) have bonded as their mothers have. Since the age of three, they have been best friends in Samoa and the States. Even thousands of miles could not separate them. They roomed together during their freshman year at Point Loma Nazarene University and both graduated in 1996.

Acknowledgments

We are indebted to:
- Dr. Jarrell Garsee, Mrs. Polly Appleby, Mrs. Joy Johnson, Mrs. Gail Dooley, and others for their contributions in helping us tell this story.
- The friends who perused the manuscript and gave us good suggestions: Dorothy Johnson, Lynda Rhoades, and Betty Thompson; Mary Ruth Sapp in California; Mary Bennett in Kansas; Judy Robertson in Arizona; the ladies Bible study group in Brush, Colorado; and the Alpha and Omega writing group.
- Rev. and Mrs. Duane Rensberry for express mailing the manuscript from Nicaragua and their encouraging words.
- The many who have prayed for us, for without them the book would not have been completed.

Introduction

It was
My last Bible school at Neiafu,
My last time on the island of Savai'i,
My last week in Samoa.
We were phasing out as career missionaries in the
    Samoas—
Something we had worked and prayed for, for 20
    years.
I was ready for furlough, but I wasn't ready to say
    good-bye to Samoa for the last time.
This definitely was a bittersweet experience.

My thoughts were focused on
One of our early trips to the village of Neiafu—
Our first Samoan wedding.
Seven cows had been killed for the occasion.
When I couldn't find our children, someone point-
    ed them out to me.
Far away from our feast,
Far away from the mats where we sat,
The kids were looking at some rocks,
Staring at all the cows' discarded insides.
An interesting experience for children straight from
    the States.

Back to the now.
I heard the children singing as they came to Sunday
    School in Neiafu.

"Sau ta o ma a'u, i le maota o lo'u tama, o i ai le
    fiafia.
Come and go with me to my Father's house,
To my Father's house, to my Father's house.
Come and go with me to my Father's house
Where there's joy, joy, joy."*

There was joy in my Father's house in Neiafu that
    morning.
There was joy in my heart as I thought of all the
    miracles God had performed.
That morning was the time I believe the Lord gave
    me the title for this book.

The miracles we share with you are not only our
    miracle stories.
They are yours too.
You see, for 20 years you put
Food on our table,
Clothes on our children's backs,
Size 14 shoes on our son John.
Thank you, my fellow Nazarenes.
Thanks for the part you have played in providing
The joy, love, and peace
In "my Father's house"
In Samoa.

—Francine Duckworth

*Words by Thoro Harris

1

Come and Go with Me

FRANCINE DUCKWORTH, MISSIONARY

The long-awaited communication arrived. We ripped open the envelope and pulled out the telegram, devouring and absorbing its contents. "Mr. and Mrs. Larry Duckworth. Stop. Congratulations! Stop. You have been appointed to Western Samoa. Stop."

We were finally appointed!

We had prepared to be missionaries for many years. The Church of the Nazarene mission department had known for some time that we felt called to missions. We had met all the requirements: attending mission school, taking tests, submitting applications and recommendations. We had been thoroughly screened by the World Mission Division and interviewed by the general superintendents. We were waiting—*impatiently* waiting!

Now, we were going to Samoa—the best-kept secret in the South Pacific. Come and go with me where the breeze, blowing through coconut palms and pua trees, keeps time with the rise and fall of the ocean tide. This island paradise is located on a map of the Pacific Ocean by drawing a line from Hawaii

Samoa's seacoast

to New Zealand. Samoa lies just east of the international date line, about 2,000 miles south of Hawaii and 1,800 north of New Zealand. The average temperature is 70-90 degrees Fahrenheit. June through September are the driest months with strong, gusty trade winds. December through March the climate is warm and moist with heavy rainfall.

After receiving the telegram that changed our lives, we traveled 8,000 miles with four children in a Datsun pickup to conduct 53 deputation services. Our last services were in California. Larry, the kids, and I said good-byes to our families and flew 5,000 miles away. Danelle, age 3; James, 5; John, 8; and Deborah, 9, were excited and sad at the same time. Just three days before flying to Samoa, James developed a rash. The doctor checked him and disclosed, "Your son has chicken pox."

We wondered what we should do. "Pray," Larry implored. God answered prayer, James had the mildest case of chicken pox on record, and the rash vanished. We boarded the plane as planned and met people in Hawaii as scheduled.

Upon arriving in Samoa on the island of Tutuila, we sensed the Polynesian's warmth and hospitality. We felt at home immediately. Conley Henderson, mission director, and Alvin Orchard, principal of the Nazarene Bible College, greeted us. The Masalosalos, one of the church families, took us to our new home, a house Nazarenes had built with Alabaster funds.

Now, I *was* in Samoa,
and I *was* the stranger.

Traveling the two miles to the church's one-acre plot, with the breathtaking view of the South Pacific, we knew this was God's place for us. At the church, James tore off his shoes and shirt and climbed a coconut tree. As I was trying to get him down, Utouto Masalosalo said, "No, don't. We can tell he is going to love Samoa. Let him be."

Conley Henderson stayed with us for a few days, providing words of encouragement and direction. He presented us with a mop and broom— and much more. "Enjoy being missionaries," he said. We knew we would.

15

It was three months before our furniture and the trusty Datsun arrived. That pickup became the Sunday School bus, often overloaded. Since Samoa is a patriarchal society, chiefs or untitled men usually sit in front and women and children ride in back. I'm still looking for a graceful way to climb in and out of the back of a pickup. We found out how to ride an aiga (family) bus to town and sleep on the floor. We were ready for anything.

Larry was called to be a missionary as a nine-year-old lad at a boys and girls camp on the Iowa District. I received my call to missions at a camp for college and high school students in southern California. At that time, I thought that people went through college and seminary, and then zipped off to the mission field. Although it may work that way for some, it certainly did not for us.

Preparation days seemed endless. During penniless times in seminary and our first pastorate in the Ozarks, in the middle of dirty dishes and diapers, I sometimes thought, *Lord, You called me to the mission field?* Later, I came to realize God's timing was perfect. He prepared us specifically for Samoa.

During missionary orientation, the presenters often talked about missionaries being strangers, that they would often be viewed as "foreign guests" and could be asked to leave at any time. Now, I *was* in Samoa, and I *was* the stranger. As I prayed, God gave this promise: "Be not afraid of their faces: for I am with thee to deliver thee, saith the LORD" (Jer. 1:8). And God was faithful. He delivered us many times. I thank the Lord for His help in every situation we faced in those early days in the South Pacific.

When we landed in Samoa, the Church of the Nazarene had been there for 17 years. Jarrell and Berniece Garsee were appointed to pioneer the denomination in this island nation. In the book *Samoa Diary*, Dr. Garsee provides a brief picture of Nazarene beginnings.

"The kingdom of heaven is like to a grain of mustard seed, which a man took, and sowed in his field: Which indeed is the least of all seeds" (Matt. 13:31-32*a*). Nearly half a lifetime ago, on a hot April morning in 1960, we arrived in America Samoa. For the next 8½ years, we endeavored to plant a tiny seed that would become a vital part of the kingdom of heaven. When we left Samoa, the young "tree" was still fragile, but

Jarrell and Berniece Garsee and children

17

there were signs of developing strength—two Samoan pastors, Vaofusi and Vaimanino; two growing Samoan Nazarene congregations, one in American Samoa and one in Western Samoa; a five-acre tract of land in the capital city of Apia in Western Samoa;* and a growing identity among both Samoans and papalagi (outlanders and foreigners). For nearly 30 years now we have watched that tree grow, sometimes up close and sometimes from a distance.

Our first Sunday in American Samoa, a child became a bit fussy during the service. I took him upstairs so his mother, Nancy, could enjoy the worship. When the tyke obviously needed his mom, she came right away. While she quieted him, I asked if she wanted to wait upstairs till the service was over.

"If you don't mind, I would like to go back downstairs and listen," she responded. "It has been over a year since we have had a pastor, and longer since we have had a resident missionary. I need some spiritual food." Nancy was nine years old when the Church of the Nazarene opened in Samoa.

NANCY FUGA STEPHENSON, SAMOAN LAYWOMAN

"Come and go with me," my brother urged. "We're having a contest."

When I went to church that night, everyone

*Western Samoa became Samoa in 1997 by a constitutional amendment. In this book, the term Western Samoa will be used since the events took place prior to that date.

was singing, hugging, and praising the Lord. Rev. Garsee got up to preach. He looked like an angel from heaven to me. He was preaching about the exact things I needed to do to obey God's Word and live for Jesus. I knew my brother would probably laugh when I got home; however, when Rev. Garsee said, "If this is what you want, come down to the altar tonight. Don't wait," I went forward. Kneeling at the altar, I asked Jesus to help me live for Him. People gathered around me and prayed. They hugged me, assuring me of their prayers.

When I went home that night, I knew I had Someone who would help me for the rest of my life. This Someone would give me a joy the world could not take away—all because my brother said, "Come and go with me."

From that time, the Church of the Nazarene was where I wanted to be. I enjoyed Sunday School and quizzing and youth activities. The Garsees guided me in God's Word, showing me how to live a Christian life. I loved being involved in the church and district events.

I was excited about my faith in God and the way things were going in our local church. The news about our church was spreading to others. Eli Nofoa became the first Nazarene elder in Samoa. He met Rev. Garsee in Nu'uuli. While Eli was pastoring a Methodist church, he testified that he heard an audible voice telling him to join the Nazarenes. Several Nazarene churches were started because he joined with us. Years later, Harold Jones's Work and Witness team from Canada built a parsonage for his family at Salelesi, where the church had been started because of Eli's influence.

After high school, I didn't know what was ahead for me. The Garsees encouraged me to go to college. I took their advice, and these wonderful missionaries helped me with the paper work. Later, I received my letter of acceptance to Bethany Nazarene College (now Southern Nazarene University).

I had mixed feelings about going to college. I had never been away from home. Bethany was almost 6,000 miles away. Should I? Could I? Yes!

I had never been on a plane before and thought this was how everyone traveled. My brother and I took a military flight from Samoa to Hawaii. The plane had a few chairs and lots of cargo. When the plane turned one way, all the chairs would slide the other way; when it turned again, all the seats slid back.

I thought my brother was going all the way to Oklahoma with me, but that didn't work out. The Lord was very good to me. He promised that He would always be with me, and He was. What a wonderful experience!

I arrived at the Will Rogers World Airport in Oklahoma City. It was so huge—bigger than the bay area of my island. Not a single soul there looked familiar. I didn't know if I should sit down and cry, or jump up and down with excitement. I *did* know that I was scared.

Bresee Hall and Mrs. Ulrich are the first memories I have of Bethany Nazarene College (BNC). Many questions came my way that I could not answer, but this saint was always there for me. She sent me to a counselor for registration, and again the questions hounded me: "How will you take care of this?" "Will you have financial aid?"

When I went to the bookstore for required texts, I thought it would be like in Samoa where you just went, picked up your books, and started studying. "The books are $60. How are you going to pay for them?" the clerk asked.

Somehow Mrs. Ulrich found out. "Give me the receipt," she said, "and I will take care of this for you." She took care of that and many other things throughout my college years. At this time, the Garsees were teaching in another Nazarene college, but Jarrell's parents lived only a block from BNC, and they became my away-from-home parents.

When the first school vacation came, everyone went home, but there was no way I could go. Once again, God was there for me.

I wanted to get involved in something, so I wouldn't think about home so much. Reba Strausbaugh, my roommate, encouraged me to join a group called Teen Challenge. She told me how exciting it was to go on the street, pass out tracts, and witness to people in the inner city. I joined.

At night we went to the inner city, and I was afraid. As people came out of the movies, all I had to do was give them a tract. It went all right the first night.

The third night, I gave a tract to a man in his early 40s. If looks could kill, I would have been dead. Yet, I told the man, "God loves you."

With a bewildered expression on his face and a sound like he had something in his throat, he asked, "What do you mean God loves me? If He loves me, why is He letting this problem destroy my life? My wife just left me. I'm thinking of committing suicide."

"There is no problem too big," I replied, "that God can't take care of if we just let Him into our life." As the man asked Jesus Christ into his heart, I praised God for His love and protection. We gave the new convert information about a church home. I went to the dorm that night feeling doubly blessed by the Holy Spirit, and I shared the experience with my roommate.

As I tell this story, I'm reminded again how God took care of me then when I was a young, scared freshman. I was happy when I found Jesus as a girl. But that happiness cannot compare with the happiness I felt the night someone else found Christ because I shared a tract and the Good News.

Hmmm! Someone must be having a pillow fight, I thought, *because a lot of cotton is coming from upstairs.*

That first year in BNC, my life seemed to go from homesickness to culture shock, from passing college exams to working through different social situations. I was so unprepared for college, but God helped me.

Around Thanksgiving time, I looked out the window and saw white fluffy things falling down. *Hmmm! Someone must be having a pillow fight*, I thought, *because a lot of cotton is coming from upstairs.* Girls ran up and down the halls screaming, banging on my door. "Did you see the snow?" they asked. They took me outside, and the trees were covered with it—my first snow. When my friends heard this was my initial experience with the frozen white stuff, they were waiting for me with snowballs. I still didn't understand. "Just reach down, pick some up, and throw it back," someone encouraged me.

Such fun! Such wonderful people! Such good classes! A totally different world than what I was accustomed to.

Of course, I looked different to my classmates too. Long black hair to my waist, bronze skin, and petite size five caught their attention. During the third year, I was secretary of the International Club. One day, I was selling used books to help raise money for the club. A young man, Joe by name, walked up to me. "Hi, how are you? Where're you from?" he asked.

Later that year, we started dating, and, in time, Joe Stephenson became my husband. Bethany Nazarene College gave me not only a quality education, special times with friends, and extensive spiritual training but also a Christian husband.

2

Everything's All Right

FRANCINE

"Polly, listen to this!" Jerry said to his wife. "We can move to Western Samoa right away."

Missionary Jerry Appleby read with excitement the letter he had just received from Malietoa, the head of state, indicating that a law banning new missionaries has been lifted for a day. "But we must move quickly," he said. "Are you ready?"

"Sure, Jerry. Just give me a couple of days to pack."

A few weeks before, Jerry, accompanied by Rev. and Mrs. Harold L. Frye Sr. from Racine, Wisconsin, visited the ruler of Western Samoa. Jerry explained that Rev. Garsee had registered the Church of the Nazarene years ago with the government. Because of a law prohibiting any new missionaries from entering the country, there was no one to guide the fledgling Nazarene work. Malietoa, though gracious, made no promises; however, he did say that if Jerry applied for a resident visa to live in the country, he would remember him. Jerry once again filled out and submitted the necessary papers.

Then the unexpected letter from His Highness

arrived. God had opened doors in ways we could never imagine. In 1971, the Applebys moved over 90 miles of ocean to Western Samoa.

Polly Appleby relates the miracle of securing land, that came to be known as "God's Three Acres."

After a few months in Western Samoa, Jerry and I realized we needed to buy some property. Most of the land was communally owned by tribal chiefs and, thus, could not be purchased. I was certain the wheels would wear off the little Mini Moke, an overgrown golf cart, as Jerry looked for land week after week.

One day after prayer, we gave the total situation to God. We discussed how we knew the Lord could do anything. He literally could have someone walk off the street and tell us where there was land, if He chose to do so. On

Jerry and Polly Appleby and children

that very afternoon, the church bus driver walked in the yard. "Hey, Jerry, do you know someone who wants to buy land?" he asked.

Jerry immediately jumped up. "Yes, we do!" he shouted. In a short time, the one-acre plot was purchased, and a two-story home, including the district office, was built. Isn't God amazing?

After we moved into our new home, we felt God wanted us to pray for the adjoining two acres for a Bible college. At that time the land was not available at all. One day the Holy Spirit urged us to quietly walk around the property and through prayer claim it for the Church of the Nazarene. Only God could have cut through the miles of red tape and allow the church to buy this acreage. Today, South Pacific Nazarene Theological College (formerly Samoa Nazarene Bible College)* is located on that beautiful property in the village of Ululoloa. Many have been trained there to spread the wonderful news of salvation. What a miracle!

Six years after Garsees returned to the United States, they were invited to assist in the first session of the new Nazarene Bible College in Samoa. Jarrell and Berniece and their children were delighted to come. Dr. Garsee expressed that the work being done by the Applebys and the Hendersons had brought new size and strength to the "Kingdom

*The name of Samoa Nazarene Bible College was changed in 1997 to South Pacific Nazarene Theological College.

tree!" He knew the seven students enrolled ensured future ministry growth as well. Everything would be all right.

✳   ✳   ✳

As the Church of the Nazarene was planted in the soil of Western Samoa, Polly related another miracle story titled "When the Rain Stopped."

In the village of Ululoloa there was no church. So, along with Conley and Carolyn Henderson, we began Bible classes for neighborhood children and teens. We thought it would be a great way to get acquainted with the people.

I love rain. But *this* was ridiculous!

At Christmas, we planned a pageant. We knew the people from the whole area would come. This play would be a bit different than any they had seen before. The program would be on the lawn in front of the Bible college. There would be room for hundreds to sit on the grass. We chose Mary, Joseph, and Baby Jesus and all the other characters in the Nativity scene. The rest of the teens would be singing in the angel choir.

Everything went well until one week before the performance. It rained. I don't mean just rain. I mean torrential rains. Day and night, without stopping, it continued to rain.

I love rain. But *this* was ridiculous! The rain caused mud and small rocks to stop up our water pipes. We took a bar of soap and showered outside under the eaves of the house. We sloshed through the mud barefoot just to get to practice. But, we didn't give up. Three days before the play, it was still raining and the teens began to get worried. "What if it doesn't quit raining?" they asked.

"Oh, it will quit because God wants us to have this play," we told them.

They looked at each other, their countenances conveying, "Are these people crazy?" We would end each practice session with prayer, thanking God that He could take care of everything and stop the rain.

Time was passing, and the rain continued to pour day and night. Yet, this is one of those times when I knew that in spite of all the stumbling blocks of Satan, God was going to intervene and everything would be all right. The Lord gave me a calm assurance in spite of the storm. The day before the play, the downpour continued. We gathered for the final rehearsal and prayed, again thanking God for stopping the rain. In my heart I believed God was teaching these young people, who were new Christians, a valuable lesson on faith—that He cares about everything.

Of course, word had spread to the community that we were having the production. They watched the pouring rains. The night before the play, we went to sleep with the rain pounding on our tin roof. Sometime during the early morning darkness, I awakened to hear steady rain still coming down. All I could pray was "Lord, it's in Your hands." I fell back to sleep.

I don't know what time I awoke, but it was daylight. Suddenly, I was awed by the silence. It had stopped raining! Jerry and I jumped out of bed and ran outside, not believing what we saw. Heavy dark rain clouds covered the entire sky as far as we could see—except for one area. Directly overhead there was a clearing that looked like a circle of sunshine flooding our village. God really did stop the rain for our play. All day teens worked in amazement, gathering limbs, vines, and colorful flowers for props.

That night hundreds came with their mats to sit and watch. They, too, had heard that God had stopped the rains, and they didn't want to miss this event. The clouds looked as if they were ready to burst at any moment, but it still wasn't raining.

Not one person went away disappointed. The teens did a magnificent job. They were able to witness to their families and friends about God's love. Suddenly, during the final song, I felt a drop of rain. I knew that God's hand was about to let the rains go. On the last verse of the last song I felt several drops. Then, as the teens belted out, "O night, O night divine!" a heavenly flood fell on the crowd. The people grabbed their little ones and ran down the roads, out across the banana and cocoa plantations, to their thatched-roof homes. They were soaked to the bone, but they carried with them memories of God's gift to us that first Christmas. And the teens—well, they will always remember the day God stopped the rain.

During these miraculous times for the Applebys, Nancy and Joe came to Samoa from the United States for their wedding.

NANCY

Joe and I had a lovely wedding. Jerry and Polly Appleby from Western Samoa and Orville and Mona Swanson from American Samoa participated in the ceremony. After the big event, Joe and I went back to Bethany, where I finished my degree. There, we had our first child, a beautiful girl, Christy Leilani. Then our family returned to Samoa, my homeland.

❊   ❊   ❊

Vai Pomele, a pastor at Lefaga in Western Samoa, became quite ill. Though he had been in the hospital, they could no longer keep him hospitalized or do anything for him. Vai returned home in a weakened condition, needing a warm meal.

Sinu'u, Vai's wife, however, had no electricity, no matches, no money. How could she fix a hot meal? Three things are needed to get a fire in Samoa: a coconut husk, a young man who can run, and a neighbor with a fire. At a nearby house, the boy lights the fibers in the husk and runs home.

The night Pastor Vai went home from the hospital, it was raining. Iosefa, the young boy who stayed with the pastor's family, ran to the next house to get the fire. By the time Iosefa returned to Sinu'u's fale (house), the flame was out. He tried again. More rain. No fire.

Sinu'u saw some men coming from the plantation and asked them, "E iai sau afi?" (Do you have any matches?)

"Ioe, ae ua susu." (Yes, but they are wet.)

The woman was exhausted, Vai needed a warm meal. She went inside the church and prayed. "Lord, You know what we need, and I guess it will take a miracle to get it." She felt impressed by the Lord to go stand near an old, gnarled tree. She obeyed.

Suddenly, lightning struck the tree. God provided the needed fire, and Sinu'u could give her husband a warm meal. Vai was soon well and pastored there until he was called to a church in Hawaii.

In 1980 Dr. Garsee held a revival in Hawaii for two Samoan congregations and the English-speaking congregation of Honolulu First Church. He preached one night in English and the next night in Samoan at Vai's church. Jarrell noted with joy how wide the branches of the growing Kingdom tree were now reaching. "The news that Rev. Pomele had been called back from the Samoan church he planted in Hawaii to be the district superintendent in Samoa reminded us of the advance of the kingdom," Dr. Garsee wrote. "It also reminded us powerfully of the days while we were in Samoa that Vai and his family had come to the Lord in our little mustard-seed church plant there."

Rev. Pomele baptizing Leilani Stephenson

Pastor Vai teaching children

**Vai and Sinu'u Pomele with
General Superintendent Eugene Stowe.**

Vai was the first Samoan district superintendent and served in that office until he retired. He
went to heaven a few years ago. Sinu'u is now living in Hawaii.

FRANCINE

Larry and I both knew that one of a missionary's first tasks is to learn the language. We started
by taking 60 one-hour language lessons. We had
been sent to reopen the church in Nu'uuli in American Samoa.

The Stephensons and others were so happy we
had come. In our first term, Larry went from pastoring that one church to being mission director,
district superintendent, and principal of the Bible
college as well.

It was time to start practicing for White Sunday. The second Sunday in October is the big day—Christmas, Children's Day, and Rally Day all rolled into one.

NANCY

When the first missionaries came to Samoa, adults were taught to read the Bible. Children were not allowed to come to church. In the beginning days of Christianity in Samoa, not much clothing was worn. The children wore nothing until they reached puberty.

When missionaries began working with children, they brought them together to study God's Word in sessions much like Vacation Bible School. Later, a program was planned for the children to recite memory verses and to act out different Bible stories. The missionaries felt the children should be clothed in front of the church to present their recitations. White material was the only color they had in sufficient quantity for everyone. Thus, their special day of recitations was originally called White Sunday for Children (not to be confused with White Sunday or Whit Sunday as observed in other Christian traditions). Eventually, the words "for children" were dropped, as all young people were involved.

During the White Sunday services, all children and any unmarried adult participated. They take charge of the entire program. One of the young people preaches. In the afternoon service, each family does a presentation. Best of all for the children, they get to eat first. To top it off, they enjoy ice cream, a special treat.

The Duckworths on White Sunday

The whole country is abuzz in anticipation for this special day. Shops have ordered in advance to be ready so everyone can have a new outfit. White shoes, dresses, shirts, and pants line the windows of every store in town. Everyone is dressed in white.

FRANCINE

We prayed and worked. We didn't want this White Sunday just to be recitations and plays. We wanted a service where someone would find the Lord. The stage was set. We practiced and rehearsed three plays: the lost coin, the lost sheep, and the lost son.

Falesiva, Nancy's brother-in-law and a prisoner, was given permission to come and see his chil-

The Stephensons on White Sunday

dren's program. For many years Nancy had prayed and shared with him about God's love, but nothing seemed to affect him. But on this White Sunday, when the prodigal son drama was ending, real pig food was carried to the platform. Larry stepped up and began speaking. "Are you tired of living in the pigpen? Do you want to come to the Father?"

Falesiva did not hesitate; he knew he was tired of living in the pigpen of his own creation. He walked to the altar and into the arms of the Heavenly Father. Nancy sat there and praised the Lord. For some time since she returned from college, there had been no pastor and no Sunday School. Church members were struggling just to keep the church open. Nancy's days back in Samoa were not

Falesiva

like her fun-filled college days. After being in the United States for four years, she sometimes felt like a foreigner with her own friends and family. After she and Joe had settled in Samoa, both their mothers had died.

Everything seemed worth it, though, when on this red-letter day Falesiva came to the Lord. Everything was going to be all right in her Father's house. God was working right in her own family.

White Sunday. Yes, it's a children's day. Yes, it's special. Yes, programs are worked on for months. Yes, families come to church that never return during the year. But, sometimes someone comes back home and gets right with the Heavenly Father. Praise the Lord, everything's all right!

3
Where There's Joy

FRANCINE

Larry stepped into the fresh water pool. The choir sang softly from the black, lava rocks behind him. It was time to baptize the 12 candidates who had requested this sacred rite. The waves of the beautiful South Pacific gently lapped up on the white, sandy beach.

The dozen individuals, dressed in white, formed a line while the other 200 youth settled themselves by the seashore, sitting on rocks or on the sand or in the shade. Friends waited with towels as the new believers stepped out of the water dripping wet, feeling bathed in God's love.

"Prayer does not prepare you for greater Christian work. Prayer is the greater Christian work."

When the 12 had been baptized, there was still a line. One by one, they came, joining the others. Yes, these young people were saved, and they wanted to live for Jesus. People kept coming. Before the service was dismissed, 56 had been baptized. Some from the choir, others from the congregation—all wanting to make an outward confession of what had happened in their heart. "I have never felt the Holy Spirit's presence like that before," Larry said, "and I may never feel Him like that again. But today He came."

Larry and I felt this youth camp held in the village of Falelima was the turning point in our work in Samoa. This camp was different. No doubt the reason was because a small group of campers gathered every morning to pray.

I read somewhere, "Prayer does not prepare you for greater Christian work. Prayer is the greater Christian work."

That was certainly the case at this camp two decades ago. Bible studies were held each morning and quizzing every afternoon. Basket-weaving contests and volleyball were the favorite daily activities. All the while, the small group continued to pray that the Holy Spirit would come. And He did! God's presence saturated the evening services.

There is still joy in the Falelima church. Just before we left Samoa in 1996, I conducted Bible schools in each of the 10 churches, including Falelima. This congregation registered over 50 children for the big event.

One day I was trying to find balloons for one of our games. I usually bought supplies in the village where our activity was held, but after going to six stores and no balloons, I thought, *Maybe I should have brought them with me.*

When one store owner said, "It isn't Christmas," I wondered if balloons are only for yuletide celebrations in Samoa.

Presto! Makeshift water balloons out of sandwich bags.

I went to bed that night thinking about my dilemma: *How we could make water balloons with no balloons?* At 5 A.M., the idea came. *That's it! Thank You, Lord,* I rejoiced inwardly.

The snack we had purchased for that day came in little plastic bags. We emptied all 60 of them in a big dishpan and covered the contents till snack time. We filled the pouches with water. Matau'a, a church member that lived next door, gave us strips of material to tie the tops. Presto! Makeshift water balloons out of sandwich bags.

For years to come, the people in Falelima will play this game with joy. For years to come, I pray they will also remember—with joy—the Bible lessons about the truthfulness of Joseph and the faithfulness of Daniel.

❊   ❊   ❊

The Nazarenes at the Saleaula Church needed a pump organ. Not just an organ, but a *pump* organ. Since there was no electricity in that part of the village, instruments requiring electricity would be of no value. The congregation had a new building, an altar, and pulpit. But nothing to provide musical accompaniment. Therefore, Conley Henderson asked us to pray about this urgent need.

Larry and I gathered our children each evening for devotions and prayed. We asked the Lord— somehow, someway—to provide a pump organ for the Saleaula people. Night after night after night we brought this petition to God.

Three weeks later, I received a telephone call from Shirley, a friend in California. "Francine, can you use a pump organ?"

The Duckworth family

"How . . . how did you know?" I stammered. "Who . . . who told you?"

The story unfolded as my friend responded. She had gone to a garage sale. Spying a large, black suitcase-type box, she asked the owner what it was. When the mysterious case was opened, it revealed a pump organ. "I have some missionary friends in Samoa," Shirley remarked, "and if they need it, I'll buy it."

"If they can use it, then I'll give it to them," the owner offered.

How interesting, I thought. *My Lutheran friend went to a Baptist minister's garage sale, and he was willing to donate to Nazarenes his pump organ, the very thing we had been praying for.*

That night, our family assembled as usual for family prayer. When I told them of Shirley's call, I asked, "Now who do you think told her, some 5,000 miles away, that we needed a pump organ?"

Four-year-old Danelle raised her hand and said joyfully, "I know, Mommy. God did!" And all our children agreed, "God did!"

What a miracle for our children to experience! Because of their persistent prayers, the Lord provided exactly what the church at Saleaula needed.

✳ ✳ ✳

Danelle adored animals. All creatures, no matter if sporting feather, furs, or scales, gave our four-year-old daughter abounding joy.

One day, she made a bed behind our house for

a chicken she found. She put down her lavalava (two yards of bright, flowered material used by females and males for various purposes), covered it in grass, and waited.

I explained that her hoped-for pet would not stay in the nest unless it was tied up or penned in, that she should not be disappointed if it was not there the next morning. (In Samoa chickens run loose, and the meat is considered more important than eggs.)

At this time, Larry had gone to Western Samoa to teach at the Bible college. He had left us some money for groceries and other necessities. I must not have been a wise steward, because I soon discovered that we had no money for eggs—for an entire week.

The next morning, Danelle ran downstairs to check out her feathered friend. She rushed back into the kitchen, proudly carrying an egg, the first one the chicken had laid. More surprised than my little girl, I put the precious treasure in the fridge.

The next morning, another egg. The following morning, another egg. Another day, another egg. For the entire week, Danelle found an egg each day. When I scrambled them, we ate them with gusto and joy.

Before that egg-filled week, we had never seen that chicken before. And we never saw it again. Yet, our family rejoiced at God's provision—just one of the many miracles Danelle and our children experienced in how the Lord took care of us on the mission field.

✳ ✳ ✳

"Come and go with me to my Father's house (Sau ta o ma a'u, i le maota o lo'u tama, o i ai le fiafia) where there's joy, joy, joy."

What joy to see the children's expressions as they came, so expectant, so ready. Their faces were scrubbed, hair fixed, teeth brushed. Dressed in their Sunday best, they walked to church. Not many cars traveled this road. None of the church members had a car, so everyone strolled along the hot, dusty road. Coconut trees and colorful hibiscus lined the sides of the road. The children's dogs followed them as they worked their way through the paths.

As the people arrived for Sunday School, they sat on the mat spread over a coral floor. Chickens ran in and out; dogs rested under the altar. The animals bothered no one, for the folks had come to learn about Jesus.

Neiafu is the farthest church from the district center, the farthest church from Apia, the capital city. As the children were coming I thought, *I have come quite a distance myself for Bible school and this Sunday service.*

That morning I had ridden the ferry for an hour. When it was time for us to disembark, I looked for the bus that would take me two hours to Neiafu. Horns honked. Motors hummed. Children hollered, selling food for the trip. Everyone was in a hurry to get on a bus. There wouldn't be another one till evening and maybe not until the next day. The buses in Samoa carry everything from people and lumber to pigs and produce. The sign in the bus reads "Capacity—33." One time Larry counted 83.

I found my bus. What a beautiful drive to Neiafu even though I had someone on my lap and a basket of taro under my feet. The hibiscus and pua in full bloom were magnificent.

We passed the blowholes where seawater rushes in, crashes against the craggy rock cliffs, and then gushes up like a geyser. They reminded me of Old Faithful in Yellowstone National Park.

Music blared. The song was "Jingle Bells," even though the month was July.

On our way, the coconut plantation on the right goes on and on. Before a devastating hurricane in 1992, Samoa's biggest export was coconut. Now many of the trees lay over on their sides, never to bear again.

We paused to let cows cross the road to "greener pastures." We stopped again—this time at a family member's house to leave a package from New Zealand. All mail delivered, we maneuvered through a long stretch of pasture and hurried on to different villages, dropping off passengers along the road. Music blared. The song was "Jingle Bells," even though the month was July. We left people at the village of Falelima where we have a church. I waved to the pastor and his wife in the yard. Some of the women were painting the rocks white to decorate the front of the church. Young boys were "mowing" the grass with the machete, a most useful tool here in the tropics. It must be workday at Falelima.

Almost to Neiafu, I wanted to pull the cord at the right place. I didn't want to stop any sooner than I had to, because I knew the walk to the church would be a mile. Ropati, one of our members from Falelima, was going to Neiafu. I got in the back of the pickup and rode the rest of the way. They were happy I had come; I was overjoyed to be there.

They have not always had joy in this congregation. The layman who gave his land for the church was no longer allowed to be on the village council nor even able to live in the small town because the Church of the Nazarene was meeting in his house. No running water there—only the rainwater that came off the roof into barrels.

In February 1992, when the hurricane named Ioane bashed Samoa, the pastor and his family lost their home and all their possessions. Neighboring families suffered the same. The 150-mile-per-hour winds blew the church down. When the pastor's house collapsed, they ran through driving rain toward the cement water tank. Ioane's ferocious force, using a big lava rock as a projectile, hammered a large hole in the wall of the tank and drained it. The gigantic container, now empty, provided shelter for many. Some men huddled in the lee of the nearby stone fence.

When the storm was over, nearly every roof

had blown away. As people started to rebuild, an interesting phenomenon happened: those who had no iron roofing, only thatch before the storm, now had a roof of salvaged iron. While those who formerly had iron now had none, and the leaves from which to make thatch had been destroyed.

The church and the parsonage at Neiafu were destroyed by that hurricane. The people and pastor carried on in makeshift wooden lean-tos. Our district Work and Witness team, local people from other villages, came and helped rebuild the church that we were worshiping in that day.

The joy, peace, and love that was felt in "my Father's house" that morning was real. Neiafu is where I heard the song. It's where I thought of the title for this book and where I wish I could take each Nazarene. Such indescribable joy!

The people at Neiafu need prayer. It's not an easy place to serve. It's not an easy place to live. It's not an easy place to share the gospel. But there is abounding, unspeakable joy!

4

Where There's Love

FRANCINE

Ululoloa Church, with just a tin roof and a cement floor at first, was built on the college campus by a Canadian Work and Witness team, headed by Harold Jones. But soon it could no longer hold all of us. The church was growing. The district was growing. The college was growing.

In the past, when there was no land, someone prayed, and God's Three Acres was acquired. When there was no church, someone prayed, and a Work and Witness team came. Therefore, when a larger building was needed, we prayed.

James Johnson, now mission director, felt God wanted him to finish as much as he could of a five-year building plan. Therefore, many gave sacrificially of their time. Missionaries, Work and Witness participants, and local people completed almost all of the buildings during a four-year period. The land the Applebys prayed for, acquired by a miracle, is now home to a beautiful, commodious campus. All a part of God's plan for "my Father's house."

*   *   *

Peni Fakaua taught our children in Sunday School while we lived in American Samoa. In 1981

James and Joy Johnson and their family

after the Johnsons came to the islands, James performed the marriage ceremony of Peni and Talisua. Then, both families moved to Western Samoa.

Peni worked as a policeman while taking classes at the Bible college. World Mission dollars, James's mentoring, and Peni's determination earned him bachelor's and master's degrees at the Nazarene seminary in the Philippines. In school Peni thought, *Lord, how are you going to help us through this?* Other students thought he was climbing coconut trees to show them how it was done. In reality, he was doing it to feed his family when there was nothing else in the house to eat.

Peni came back to Samoa. While pastoring the

Ululoloa Church and teaching at the college, he became president of Samoa Nazarene Bible College, the first Samoan to hold that position.

Little by little, day by day, with hard work and prayer, a miracle was unfolding in front of our eyes. God led Peni from policeman to professor to pastor and then to president.

After returning to the States, I placed a long-distance call to Mrs. Fakaua in Samoa. The connection was good, with minimal static. Phone lines had certainly improved in the more than two decades since we first arrived in Samoa.

"Francine, I'm sewing uniforms," Talisua said. "The choir is singing on national television. Things are going well."

I put the receiver down and prayed for all of our people there. *When we went to Samoa,* I reflected, *there were people who lived in the same village that didn't even know where the Nazarene Church was or what it stood for. Now we are on national TV. Praise the Lord!*

❊ ❊ ❊

Work and Witness teams that came to Samoa made an impression on us and our families. They brought tools, food, money, skills, materials, and lots of love to build buildings and relationships. For example, Gail Bennett felt love for "my Father's house" in Ottawa, Kansas, and spread that love all the way to Lotopa Church of the Nazarene in Western Samoa.

In 1986 we furloughed in Olathe, Kansas. Our teens John, James, and Danelle were asked to talk about missions with the Ottawa youth group. There was an instant bond with our family and their church. Several felt God's call to go to Samoa on a Work and Witness project.

As the painters continued,
the Lord stretched the paint.
The project was finished—on time!

Gail, a teenager, prepared for almost two years. The Ottawa church organized numerous fund-raisers for their project of rebuilding a church and parsonage. Gail watched as these godly people faithfully pulled from their savings and sacrificed to give to others. Each week they met and prayed for God's direction. Gail believes those prayers brought their team together and allowed the Lord to prepare them for His service.

"Once in Samoa," Gail said, "we had devotions three times a day and surrounded ourselves with prayer. We were dependent on God for everything—safety, health, food, travel, money, supplies, translator, and more."

Members of the team were everywhere, fixing the noon meal, working on the roof, painting walls. When the paint ran low, there was no money to buy more. Workers came down from the roof, and cooks left their duties in the open-air kitchen. Everyone gathered inside the church, prayed, and returned to work. As the painters continued, the Lord stretched the paint. The project was finished—on time!

"My life was changed by seeing God's hand directly moving in my life and others," Gail wrote. "It seemed too good to be true that God would be so attentive and caring to a silly 16-year-old girl like me."

While Gail was in Samoa, I was privileged to be her missionary mom, and we hosted her 16th birthday celebration. When she returned to Ottawa, her wonderful memories of Samoa and missionaries were never far away. Many letters traveled back

Gail and Scott Dooley and daughter

and forth over the ocean. She knew that God was using the correspondence to direct her life. Little did Gail know how much the Lord was using her to encourage us.

At the age of 18, Gail responded to Missionary Johnson's biblical challenge to go to all Judea and Samaria and to the ends of the earth, making disciples of all nations. "The Lord spoke loud and clear to me and asked if I would be willing to go to the ends of the earth," she confesses. "I gladly said yes!"

Gail enrolled in the nursing program at Mid-America Nazarene University. There, she met and married Scott Dooley, also called to missions.

Preparation is difficult for this dedicated couple. Scott recently graduated from medical school. Gail, a nurse and mother, says that God continues to direct and use them as they wait for the right place and time to do what God has called them to do. While they wait patiently, Gail is grateful for the love she discovered in "my Father's house" in Samoa.

5

Where There's Peace

FRANCINE

The Book Room, a peaceful place consisting of one little air-conditioned room, was the only Christian bookstore in American Samoa. We knew it was needed when we couldn't find an English or Samoan Bible anywhere. Yet, we could find *Newsweek* and *Playboy* and any other secular magazine or book imaginable.

Through the Book Room, the Lord taught me a valuable lesson. He wanted us to take what we had, and He would make it what He wanted it to be.

Books and magazines were popular items. Women at retreats often purchased more than $300 of stock. Book stands placed on the dock when cruise ships came in provided people good material to buy and read during their travels.

In Nu'uuli where we lived and worked for almost seven years, village children would come by the Book Room and buy a top or a book with scripture. Methodist pastors came to Larry for Bibles to use as prizes. Catholic sisters came for music tapes. Assemblies of God missionaries bought texts for classes at their Bible college. Seminary students from the Congregational church bought holiness sermon outlines and preached from them. Dozens of youth came through this extension of "my Father's house" for Bible story hour.

Her faced glowed when she opened the Bible and read John 3:16 in her own language.

When our daughter Deborah was a senior at Samoana High School, she worked in the Book Room, and many of her friends would come by and visit. They would sit and read and buy books. One day a friend of Deborah's came by and shared a problem. While there, she asked Jesus to forgive her sins, and He helped her with the difficult situation, giving her marvelous peace.

Tuli, a 9-year-old girl, came to story hour, Bible school, and everything we had to offer. Since she was Tongan, we ordered some Tongan Bibles. Her faced glowed when she opened the Bible and read John 3:16 in her own language. Tuli now attends a university in Boston.

Does she remember the peace she found in the Book Room at the age of 9 or the Bible stories of David and Daniel she heard at the age of 10? What about the Bible school when she made a total commitment to God at the age of 12?

I believe she does remember. I believe the people won to the Lord, the children that were taught God's love, and everyone that bought His Word were drawn closer to the Living Lord as they walked through the doors of the Book Room, the only Christian bookstore for 30,000 people.

Sure, there were frustrations. Break-ins. Stolen books. "Permanently borrowed" Bibles. We wondered why 5,000 Bibles were left on the wharf for days before officials released them to us. But God was at work on this island with a handful of people. His Word was going out and would not return to Him void.

When our family moved to Western Samoa, as manager of the Book Room, I would go back once a month to process books and order needed materials.

One day bookstore volunteers phoned me. A shipment of Bibles from Fiji had been in for several days, and the duty was $500. The Book Room did not have that amount of money. We needed a miracle—right away. All involved interceded earnestly, and the Lord gave us His peace. Larry flew to American Samoa to visit with officials. He explained what we were trying to do in the islands and for their people. By afternoon the Bibles were delivered—no duty paid!

NANCY

I observed the small, struggling church in Nu'uuli grow. I rejoiced as many of my extended family accepted Christ and joined the Church of the

Nazarene. I watched as other churches were started in Western Samoa.

Then in 1985, my family moved to Illinois. We found a Church of the Nazarene. We worked with Caravan, a scouting-type program for children, as Francine had introduced us to Caravan in Samoa. She had started with one Pathfinder book and six girls ages 9 to 11. In America, we had much more than that and began our "mission" work in Illinois.

Kingdom dollars invested in Samoa have resulted in Kingdom building in the United States.

For some time I had been wondering what I could do for Samoans in the States. We visited the Duckworths during their furlough year in Olathe, Kansas. As Francine and I prayed together, I knew God had a plan. Leaving Olathe, I picked up a promise card in the car that spoke to my heart. It was the Lord's way of telling me that my time to serve Him would come. I was at peace.

Later, when we moved to California, we learned quickly what "services" would be needed. We directed the children's quizzing program at a small Church of the Nazarene in Santa Ana. We had observed how it was done while in Illinois. Our little church won at both the district and regional levels. How exciting for our congregation, with many children speaking English as a second language, to beat the eight-year champs!

As I went to Samoan meetings on the United States west coast, I tried to encourage other Samoan workers from Long Beach to San Francisco to Seattle. I even preached on Sundays. Remembering that little scripture promise card I found in the car one day, I believed this was my time to serve. I felt that the Lord wanted me to take the ministerial course of study. I pastored the Samoan Church of the Nazarene in Santa Ana for six years until October 1997.

Some Nazarenes may think if their dollars are sent to Samoa they will reach only the people in Samoa. I would like for my denomination to consider this. I found the Lord in Samoa through Nazarene missions. And as I have lived and worked in America, my family and I have done some of the same things the missionaries did for us. Kingdom dollars invested in Samoa have resulted in Kingdom building in the United States.

FRANCINE

The move to Western Samoa in 1986 was difficult for me. Deborah had left for Point Loma Nazarene College (now University) the year before, and that was hard. But this latest move just six months before furlough when John was a junior in high school was also hard. Though it was the same people group, it was a very different country. Western Samoa is an independent country with an annual income per capita of less than $800, while American Samoa is a United States Territory. In addition, our children had to enroll in a different school, live in a different village, and attend a different church.

American Samoa was truly home for our children. John remembered the trips to Pago Bay "to see the lights." He had fond memories of riding the bus that stopped at the bakery where anyone could get off and buy fresh, hot bread with one-fourth or one-half pound of butter. Back on the vehicle, we would pull the loaf apart and dab it in the butter—a yummy snack for the rest of the ride to town. Sometimes we would share with the Samoans. Sometimes they would share with us. What fond memories for an 8-year-old who had traveled 5,000 miles across the Pacific.

Now John was almost 17. Missionary families seem to have fun times, even if their dads' passports have 22 stamps or their moms are busily involved with women's and children's ministries. Would God help us to have some special times during this move? Through these times? Yes, He would. Yes, He did.

Once, James came home from school. "We're lucky, aren't we?" he declared. That particular day I was not feeling lucky or blessed, but I decided to hear him out.

"We have screens on our windows and running water," he went on. He had been at several friends' houses who had neither. In a third-world country, screens and running water are luxuries along with other things we take for granted in the States.

Yes, James, we are blessed, I thought. I knew God was helping our children and our family through this move; He would help us as we lived in this country and served Him.

During our furlough in 1986, Jarrell Garsee held a revival for Filipo Robertson, pastor of the Samoan church in Long Beach, California. "What a delight!" he wrote. "There we met the families of many who had first begun their association with the Church of the Nazarene in the mustard-seed days of our time in Samoa."

Back in Western Samoa after furlough, we lived in the village of Ululoloa. Larry was mission treasurer, evangelism coordinator, and Bible college teacher.

The Johnsons were on furlough. One miracle happened for them just before they left. Their son James fell in a cesspool in the backyard. No one was around except his friend Leatapo, a son of a Bible college student. Leatapo heard the cry for help and found James's mother, Joy, who quickly rescued James. God is good, and He faithfully cares for His children around the world.

I was on the road again
with my big, black trunk
and literature.

We opened an extension of the Book Room in Western Samoa, located in the district office across the street from the Mormon temple. Talisua, our secretary, was asked "What are you doing right across the street from the temple?"

"Telling people about Jesus," she responded.

A table was placed outside the office with books, Bibles, and scripture-related articles. As buses stopped and the dust flew, people would come and look and buy. We handed out hundreds of copies of the *Herald of Holiness*, *World Mission*, *Standard*, and other holiness literature, which churches in the States had sent to us. The Lord knew some of these people could not buy reading material. He also knew that I would never be able to go to some of the outer villages.

God's lesson was more clear to me than ever. "Take what I have given you, and I will help you make it what I want it to be." We didn't have a bookstore in Western Samoa, but we did bring some of our inventory to the island knowing God had a plan. I could have said we don't have a building, not even a room, and we can't do anything. But I remembered what God had taught me in American Samoa. I took what I had—a trunk full of Bibles, special-day program books, commentaries, magazines, and other books—and started out. People were hungry for God's Word.

I was on the road again with my big, black trunk and literature. This time to the large Wesleyan bookstore in Apia. Yes, the manager was in. Yes, they could use some commentaries and other Christian books. In fact, they bought the rest of the stock.

* * *

In the early '80s, Liuga Faumui built a house for his family across the road from Conley and Carolyn Henderson in Ululoloa. Before the Hendersons left for the States, they contacted their new neighbors. From that contact and many prayers, Liuga's children started going to Sunday School. Va'alotu, Liuga's wife, would walk down the dirt road with her children to the different services and activities, but Liuga never had time for the Lord.

Conley and Carolyn Henderson and their children

He had important things to do. He worked for the United Nations, and many people in the government spent time with him.

One day, Liuga had a stroke and ended up in the hospital. Mica, the pastor, visited him. Later, when Liuga's children were in a church program, he went to see his kids perform.

In the meantime, the Johnsons moved into the mission house close to the Faumuis. The two families shared cookies and visited back and forth. Liuga kept coming to the services, sensing God's peace and joy. Finally, he accepted Christ and committed his life fully to the Lord.

Remember Polly Appleby and those few Bible college students who walked around an acre of land and claimed it for the Lord? That property is where Liuga and his family became followers of Christ. How grateful we are that the Applebys and others prayed in faith for a miracle, that the Hendersons contacted the Faumuis, that the Johnsons visited them, that Nazarenes gave faithfully to world missions, sharing God's joy, love, and peace with others.

Soon after, Liuga was sent to Bangladesh as a United Nations' representative. How sad we were to see him and part of his family leave.

Liuga and Va'alotu Faumui arrived in Bangladesh. As he strolled the streets, he thought, *These people have many needs. The Church of the Nazarene could help here.* But the church wasn't registered in Bangladesh. With the Lord in his heart and Church of the Nazarene on his mind, Liuga started some

Bible studies. Today, the Church of the Nazarene is registered in Bangladesh. During the 1993 General Assembly, a pastor and representative from Bangladesh attended.

Next, Mr. Faumui was sent to another country in Asia where the Church of the Nazarene had not yet entered. Due to his influence, Nazarenes are now working in this Creative Access country through Compassionate Ministries.

Following this assignment, Liuga was appointed to Pakistan, an area where there is little peace. During our 1991-92 furlough, Larry often told Liuga's story during deputation services. At the beginning of the furlough, he asked people to pray for Liuga and his family as the church was not registered in Pakistan. Halfway through the year, Larry read the Nazarene *Weekly Summary* headline, "Church of the Nazarene Is Registered in Pakistan." The holiness influence is reaching lives in a country thousands of miles away from the South Pacific islands where God worked a miracle in Liuga's life.

As I revised this chapter, I wondered where Liuga was, where and how the Lord was using him. I called Western Samoa to find out. Liuga had been assigned to a country in the Middle East.

Liuga and his wife need our prayers. As they live for the Lord, whether in Samoa or another world area, they need Nazarenes to intercede to the Lord on their behalf. Who knows where the Church of the Nazarene will be registered next— just because a United Nations' representative, who is a Nazarene, is sharing the peace of Christ.

6

Jesus Is the Way

FRANCINE

Puipui Mata'utia and his wife, Morita, knew Jesus was the Way to "my Father's house." And they wanted to worship in the Church of the Nazarene where they knew holiness was preached.

Puipui was the customer-relations manager at the Bank of Western Samoa, where he had a staff of 115. He had worked for this financial institution for 30 years, and his daughters were employed there too. Puipui showed everyone he worked with that Jesus is the Way. What a witness this family was for God and His kingdom!

The Mata'utias and their five children—Juanita, Ofa, Monica, Peiati, and Wesley—were faithful to their church. They helped in invaluable ways—picking up people for services, singing specials, playing the piano, teaching Sunday School, and serving on the church board. They sincerely desired to live a holy life and to worship with people who shared a Wesleyan theology.

Puipui was also active on the district level as a member of the Advisory Board and college board. This dedicated layman always tried to do what was best for the church and its members.

One day, when Puipui was playing volleyball

at a youth camp, he had a heart attack. The doctor warned him, "Mr. Mata'utia, you cannot do as much as you did before. You can work at the bank or you can work at the church, but you can no longer do both."

"If I can't do both, I will work with the church." And that is what Puipui did.

He drove his own van for the church. Sunday after Sunday he picked up Faigafou, one of the members who had palsy. Puipui continued to teach Sunday School and lead the teen group. He was always available to help Work and Witness teams, chauffeuring them around the island.

He was like an uncle to our sons—encouraging and mentoring them. Puipui modeled for John and James the biblical way to solve problems and work things out.

Yes, Puipui knew Jesus was the Way when he came to the Church of the Nazarene and also pointed others to that way.

The last time I saw Puipui and his wife, Morita, we had asked them if they would be field coordinators for the Child Sponsorship Program for Nazarene Compassionate Ministries, which would assist pastors' kids. When we went to the bank to get cards signed, Puipui promised, "If we can do something to help these children, I am certainly willing."

After 20 years as a Nazarene missionary, working with Samoans in the islands and in the States, I'm convinced "my Father's house" is in good hands with laypeople, such as Puipui and his family, who show Jesus is the Way.

* * *

Tala'ifua, better known as Fua, knows Jesus is the Way to "my Father's house." She grew up in a Methodist minister's home. She has faithfully pointed others to His way, living and working for Christ in the village of Falelima on the island of Savai'i.

One time when I was with Fua, she demonstrated His peace—His way—in a beautiful, remarkable way. Many women were going by boat to the island of Upolu for a big Mother's Day celebration. Everyone was looking forward to the festivities. Mothers from all over the island had gathered on the pier to board the ferry.

I lived only one-fourth mile from the wharf, so it was easy for me to walk down at four o'clock in the morning to get in line. Other Nazarene women, who had arrived early, were waiting. Some women had been on a bus since 2 A.M. to be there on time.

Without fanfare, Fua stepped back and started singing.

The women sat on lavalavas spread out on the cement wharf. Since we were just behind the gate, we would be some of the first ones on—or so we thought.

As the ferry's motors started and the gate opened, the women stood up and gathered their belongings. The women behind us evidently be-

67

lieved there were more bodies than there was room on the boat. So they started pushing and shoving.

I was with 30 of our churchwomen and knew they all wanted to attend the celebration, and if we didn't get on board, we would not get there at all. This was the only boat that would take people to Upolu. The Nazarene women were some of the first ones in line, but others quickly elbowed their way ahead of us.

I looked at Fua. Without fanfare, she stepped back and started singing. What peace I observed on her face. (In my mind, I can still it see today.) Without hesitation, our churchwomen followed Fua's example; they stepped back and started singing too.

Fua

We sang. We waited. Some ladies indicated to Fua that we should get in line, which meant, of course, stepping in, pushing, shoving. She shook her head to indicate no and continued singing.

Five hundred women passed us by and boarded a ferry built for 200. What an example Fua was! What a witness the Church of the Nazarene women were that day! I was happy to be included in that group.

At the end, we did get on—and without any jostling. We had to sit on the lower level designed for cars. But I never had a sweeter ride than that one with the women who sang in the midst of chaos. It's interesting, isn't it, that the Bible says "many that are first shall be last; and the last shall be first" (Matt. 19:30). We were the last on the boat, but the first to get off and get on a bus.

Fua is one of the reasons I could leave Samoa after two decades. She has God's peace, and she is willing to share it with others. She eagerly points people to Jesus the Way. I thank God for this saintly Samoan lady.

The tiny seed that the Garsees had planted spread from American Samoa, to villages in Western Samoa, to the island of Upolu, and farther on. Fua and the Nazarene women were from Savai'i, the largest, most untouched island of the Samoas.

In 1989, Dr. Garsee was called to pastor First Church of the Nazarene in Anaheim, California. While there, he held a revival in Pupa Masalosalo's church in Santa Ana, read scripture from the Samoan Bible at the church dedication of our new

Samoan church in Wilmington, California, and prayed in Samoan the dedicatory prayer for a Samoan pastor being ordained. Berniece Garsee was reunited with several of the teenagers in her Sunday School class in Samoa, including Juanita, Pupa, Sapela, and Nancy, coauthor of this book.

"The reality of God's grace growing His kingdom hit me full-force," Dr. Garsee said, "when I was asked to speak at the Samoan pastor's conference in Orange, California, in the early 1990s. I had no idea what to expect. When I walked into the meeting, I was stunned by the presence of 24 Samoan Nazarene pastors, only three of whom I knew personally. They represented churches in Australia, New Zealand, Western Samoa, American Samoa, Hawaii, and two or three other states in America. I told them that it was wonderful to see that the tiny seed we planted had been watered by the many faithful missionaries and Samoan laborers alike, and that 'God gave the increase' (1 Cor. 3:6). And the tree's branches now cover approximately one-half of the world's diameter, and it provides shelter and salvation for so many."

The Gospel of Matthew reminds us that the mustard seed is "the least of all seeds: but when it is grown, it is the greatest among herbs, and becometh a tree, so that the birds of the air come and lodge in the branches thereof" (Matt. 13:32).

7

Will I See You There?

FRANCINE

"I am a product of World Mission," wrote Filipo Robertson, the interpreter for Jerry Appleby in American Samoa. And Filipo, with the assistance of his missionary friend, attended and graduated from Nazarene Bible College in Colorado Springs. The genial Samoan won the hearts of the America people he met and worked with. Later, upon his return to Samoa, Filipo pastored, married, and taught at Samoa Nazarene Bible College in Ululoloa.

Rev. Robertson started the Nazarene church in Solosolo. Prior to this church plant, new congregations had been started by missionaries who worked in various villages. Thus, world mission dollars invested in Filipo's education were paying off. While in Samoa, he made contacts that would play a large part in what the Lord had in store for our mission in the future.

Filipo went back to the States to enroll in Fuller Theological Seminary, and he was appointed the coordinator of Samoan Nazarene work in America. He started the Samoan church in Wilmington, California. He loved the people, and the people loved him

and his family. Just after the church had been dedi-
cated, Dr. George Rench and his wife visited Filipo.
(The late Dr. Rench was then the director of the
Asia-Pacific Region.)

"Would you be the district superintendent in
Samoa?" Dr. Rench asked.

"But we're happy here," Filipo commented.

"Would you pray about it?" George urged.
"Then, let us know."

The Robertsons did pray about it. As a family,
they felt they should return to Samoa and serve the
Lord and the Church of the Nazarene.

"One of the hardest things I've ever done is to
stand in front of that congregation in Wilmington
and tell them what we were going to do," Filipo ad-
mitted. "The congregation questioned: 'Who will
be our pastor? Who will take care of us? You built
this church. We don't want you to leave.'"

Filipo obeyed the Lord. He called Dr. Rench
and told him of his decision. The family started
packing. They bought things to take with them;
they sold and gave things away. With decisions
made and good-byes said, they returned to their
homeland after being gone for eight years. The
Robertsons were different. Samoa was different.
They knew it would take a miracle to adjust to this
new ministry assignment.

"In October 1990 our family arrived in Samoa,"
Filipo wrote. "And the work was sure cut out for
us—pastoring a church, helping pastors, meeting
budgets, encouraging people. In addition, missionaries were leaving."

Filipo's family settled in, renewed old friendships, and visited with family while Filipo pastored the English-speaking congregation. Sometimes a handful showed up; other times just the missionaries and their families. Filipo kept preaching and praying, and finally New Life Church was organized. He preached in both English and Samoan, depending on the activities and programs and depending on the crowd. During district assemblies he translated for the general superintendents.

> "I'm dying with cancer, but the Lord, Filipo and Susanna, and this New Life Church are helping me tremendously."

One night Filipo said to me, "Will I see you there? Will you come to our Sunday evening service at New Life?" Now that was a question I had asked neighbors and friends for almost 20 years.

"Sure, Filipo, I'll be there. I'll be glad to come to 'my Father's house.'"

That Sabbath night the little room, serving as the church, was filled. They were meeting in downtown Apia, where we had wanted to start a church for years. I sat beside Susanna, his wife, who told me about this one and that one: "He is from parliament. He is headmaster of a prestigious school."

Then the testimonies began. "I was away from the Lord, and Filipo visited me. I prayed last Wednesday at his Bible Study. I'm not drinking any-more."

Another person spoke: "I went back to my wife, and Filipo is helping me give my life back to the Lord."

Filipo and Susanna Robertson

A layman testified: "I'm dying with cancer, but the Lord, Filipo and Susanna, and this New Life Church are helping me tremendously. Praise the Lord!"

The late Filipo Robertson enabled our church to be on national TV and get our pastors devotional spots on radio. He spoke at the Prime Minister's Breakfast, talked at prayer meetings, and gave the devotional at an Independence Day celebration with over 50,000 people.

Yet, the Robertsons didn't always have an easy life. When money was limited, the children frus-trated at school, and patience lacking, Filipo must have wondered why he came back to his homeland. Yet, he made a difference in the lives of Samoans. I thank the Lord for Filipo, a dedicated man of God.

* * *

During our fourth term in Samoa, we lived on the island of Savai'i. No Nazarene missionary had ever lived there before. We believed God would use us to encourage our churches on the island. Our home was located in Salelologa, just a short distance from the wharf. From this house in a highly trafficked area, we were able to minister to all that came and went from the island as well as all around Savai'i.

Lino Nu'u and his family

While living in Savai'i, a major part of our job description was translation. Larry worked on the hymnal for several years. He and Lino Nu'u spent every evening from 7 to 11 preparing it for publication. Larry then began working on the Nazarene *Manual.* During our last term, the *Manual* was distributed to pastors and key laypersons. Larry's last contribution in the area of literature was getting *My Utmost for His Highest* printed in Samoan.

Each month Moasigi, our translator who was pastor of an independent church, brought his work. I typed, Larry edited, and I retyped it. Moasigi looked at it again, and then I would go back to the computer. When that month's booklet was printed and distributed, we started on the next month's. We were encouraged throughout the year as we visited churches and the pastor was using that day's thought and devotional with his family, or sharing it on the radio. At times it would even be the text for a sermon.

While Larry worked on translations, I taught a computer course for college-age girls for two reasons: to teach some life skills and to help them with their spiritual walk. Many that came to the class might never have attended church. They typed holiness devotions and scriptures from the Bible as they practiced each day. Makerita, a young lady from our church at Papa, did very well in the class and was able to get a job at the government library. She is still working there and a vital part of "my Father's house" in Papa.

* * *

As district superintendent, Filipo Robertson visited Nazarene churches on Savai'i. Once again, he asked the question, "Will I see you there in 'my Father's house'?" He had a special get-acquainted meeting in the PuleNu'u (meeting house) in Salelologa where we lived.

Some day there will be a church in that village. Will it be because Larry sat many evenings with some of the village chiefs, having tea and talking about spiritual matters? Will it be because we passed out literature in the market and various places of business? Will it be because James Johnson's college students had an open-air meeting? Will it be because Filipo came and had a get-acquainted meeting at the PuleNu'u in Salelologa? We don't know, but as Rev. Garsee planted the seed, and many have watered it, God has promised to give the increase. "My Father's house" will be established.

8

There Is Room for All

FRANCINE

Nancy was living in California; I was in Colorado. The due date for the manuscript was near. I had traveled to the west coast to see our children. Nancy and I had one day and one night to pull all the loose ends together and meet the deadline.

Early one morning, Nancy and I were hard at work on the book again. We had planned our schedule around children and grandchildren. I had been typing since 2 A.M. We were revising what we had written the night before.

We were on a mission. We had a book to write and a deadline to keep. People around the world needed to hear the story.

While I was reading, Nancy dabbed at her eye. I thought she had something in it so hurried on to the next sentence. Then I looked up. As tears trickled down her cheeks, she said, "I'm sorry, Francine, but I'm getting blessed."

"We can take time to get blessed." My voice cracked.

And we did. As we recalled past miracles, we rejoiced. We paused and praised the Lord for His goodness. We asked God to let us know what to write, so the readers—and listeners—would be just as blessed as we were in recalling God's wonders in Samoa.

NANCY

That morning with Francine, as well as countless others, I praised God for His good gifts. As I share this story, I'm reminded again how God saved me at nine years of age, kept me close to Him during my teen years, took care of me then when I was a scared freshman, and helped me through tumultuous college years. Plus, Joe and I celebrated our 27th anniversary in January of 2000.

Although we have lived in America for many years, we remembered our start in Samoa—the godly missionaries who came, the gracious Lord that answered prayer, and the host of people who responded to His outstreached arms of love.

The foundation had been built, the cornerstone laid.

Nazarenes are still earning dividends on the mission dollars they gave long ago. For six years I pastored the Samoan congregation in Santa Ana. Our daughter, Leilani, who has been a good friend with Danelle, the Duckworth's youngest daughter, graduated from Point Loma also. Leilani has a vibrant testimony of how the Lord has helped her through the years. She is now NWMS president in our local church.

FRANCINE

Larry and I had finished our last furlough year of deputation services. Some of the highlights were services in over 100 churches on 30 districts; Danelle's graduation from Point Loma Nazarene University; dedicating our two grandsons; taking Hannah May, our granddaughter, to Papa's Pizza; riding for 30 hours on the bus to Birmingham with our granddaughter Tanya; seeing people in Canada who had been on the very first Work and Witness Team to Samoa; going to James's graduation from Northwest Nazarene College (now University) one day and his wedding the next.

What a wonderful way to finish up our 20 years of work in Samoa. We had done what the World Mission Division asked us to do. We had worked ourselves out of a job.

The foundation had been built, the cornerstone laid. After two decades for us and many years for others in building "my Father's house," national laypeople were working for Him and pastors were in place. The mission director's job had been abolished, and Samoan leaders were in charge.

In the Introduction, I stated that it was kind of a bittersweet experience when Larry and I left Samoa. We were thrilled that Samoa was almost a regular district. How exciting to see our friend, Peni, who had taught our children Sunday School 20 years ago, now president of the Bible college. And Filipo, the student who finished at NBC, was now district superintendent. They were all working together to continue the building of "my Father's house."

Yet, Samoa still needs—
Those who will sing "Come and go with me,"
Ministers who faithfully preach the Good News,
Pastor's wives who share His love,
Camps where people can feel His joy,
Laypeople who tell neighbors that Jesus is the Way,
Work and Witness teams to share their skills and
Christ's peace.

Everything will be all right,
If we continue to pray and love and give
In Samoa,
In the States,
Around the world,
So all can enjoy "my Father's house" where
There is room for all.

Appendix

MISSIONARIES ASSIGNED TO SAMOA

Jarrell and Berniece Garsee (1960-68)
John and Virginia Abney (1964-65)
Jerry and Polly Appleby (1969-76)
Orville and Mona Swanson (1970-74)
Conley and Carolyn Henderson (1974-80)
Alvin and Bette Orchard (1975-80)
Larry and Francine Duckworth (1977-97)
Annette Taft Brown (1979-80)
Richard and Jane Reynolds (1980-82)
James and Joy Johnson (1981-95)
Michael and Patricia Hutchens (1985-86)
Brian and Evelyn Vanciel (1990-92)
Randy and Karen Lingenfelter (1997—present)

VOLUNTEERS TO SAMOA

Roy and Dora Brook (1979; 1988-89)
Harold and Ruth Jones (1986)
W. J. "Jay" and Judith Muse (1986)
Cliff and Vera Ingram (1986-87)
Marie Sivewright (1987)
Andrea York (1990-91)
Ronald and Neva Beech (1996-97)

WORK AND WITNESS TEAMS IN SAMOA

September 1977—Team from British Columbia, Canada, built two fales (houses), one at Lotopa and one at Ululoloa.

February 1979—Team from First Church of Spokane, Washington, built a 30' by 60' frame building in Salelesi.

January 1984—Team from Hilo, Hawaii, renovated Bible college buildings.

June 1989—Team from Ottawa, Kansas, repaired and refurbished parsonage and completed major work on the church at Lotopa.

June 1989—Team from Clarkson, Washington, led by Lawrence Bradley built new Falelima church.

August 1989—Team from Amarillo, Texas, and New Mexico built new mission house at Ululoloa.

March 1990—Team from Pasadena, California, First Church built the church on the Bible college campus at Ululoloa.

July 1992—Team from San Diego Mission Valley Church laid blocks for the Bible college administration and library building.

March 1993—Team from Baker City, Oregon, built the Papa parsonage and remodeled the Bible college dormitory.

August 1994—Canadian team, led by Roy and Dora Brook, laid blocks for the second phase of the Bible college administration and library building.

January 1995—Team from Alaska finished installing trusses and purlins on the roof.

February 1995—Team from Portland, Oregon, finished roof and continued inside work on the Bible college administration and library building.

Pronunciation Guide

aiga	ah-EE-ngah
Apia	ah-PEE-ah
Eli Nofoa	AY-lee noh-FOH-ah
E iai sau afi	ay ee-AH-ee sau AH-fee
Faigafou	fah-ee-ngah-FOH-oo
fale	FAH-lay
Fa'amanuia le atua iate outou	fah-ah-mahn-oo-EE-ah lay ah-TOO-ah ee-AH-tay oh-oo-TOH-oo
Fakaua	fah-kah-OO-ah
Falelima	fah-lay-LEE-mah
Falesiva	fah-lay-SEE-vah
Filipo	fee-LEE-poh
Fuga	FOO-ngah
Ioe, ae ua susu	ee-OH-ay AH-ay OO-ah SOO-soo
Ioane	ee-oh-AH-nay
Iosefa	ee-oh-SAY-fah
Juanita	oo-ah-NEE-tah
lavalava	LAH-vah-LAH-vah
Leatapo	lay-ah-TAH-poh
Lefaga	lay-FAH-ngoh
Leilani	lay-ee-LAH-nee
Lino Nu'u	LEE-noh NOO-oo
Liuga Faumui	lee-OO-ngah fah-oo-MOO-ee
Lotopa	loh-TOH-pah
Makerita	mah-kay-REE-tah
Malietoa	mah-lee-ay-TOH-ah
Masalosalos	mah-sah-loh-SAH-lohs
matai	mah-TAH-ee
Matau'a	mah-TAU-ah
Mica	MEE-cah
Moasigi	moh-ah-SEE-ngee
Morita	moh-REE-tah
Neiafu	nay-ee-AH-foo
Nofoa	noh-FOH-ah
Nu'uuli	noo-oo-OO-lee

Ofa	OH-fah
Pago Pago	PAH-ngoh PAH-ngoh
Papa	PAH-pah
papalagi	pah-pah-LAH-ngee
Peiati	pay-ee-AH-tee
Peni Fakaua	PAY-nee fah-KAU-ah
pua	POO-ah
Puipui Mata'utia	poo-ee-POO-ee mah-tah-oo-TEE-ah
PuleNu'u	poo-lay-NOO-oo
Pupa Masalosalo	POO-pah mah-sah-loh-SAH-loh
Ropati	loh-PAH-tee
Salelesi	sah-lay-LEH-see
Salelologa	sah-lay-loh-LOH-ngah
Saleula	sah-lay-OO-ah
Sapela	sah-PAY-lah
Savai'i	sah-vah-EE-ee
Sau ta o ma a'u	sau tah oh mah AH-oo
i le maota	ee lay mah-OH-tah
o lo'u tama	oh LOH-oo TAH-mah
o i ai le fiafia	oo ee ah-ee lay fee-ah-FEE-ah
Selaga	say-LAH-ngah
Sinu'u	see-NOO-oo
Solosolo	SOH-loh-SOH-loh
Tala'ifua	tah-lah-ee-FOO-ah
Talisua	tah-lee-SOO-ah
Tongan	TOH-ngahn or TAHN-gahn
Tuli	TOO-lee
Tutuila	too-too-EE-lah
Ululoloa	oo-loo-loh-LOH-ah
Ulrich	UHL-rich
Upolu	oo-POH-loo
Utouto	oo-toh-OO-toh
Va'alotu	vah-ah-LOH-too
Vaimanino	vah-ee-mah-NEE-noh
Vai Pomele	VAH-EE poh-MAY-lay
Vaofusi	vah-oh-FOO-see or vau-FOO-see